SPOTLIGHT ON CIVIC ACTION

WHY VOTING MATTERS

KIP ALMASY

PowerKiDS press.

NEW YORK

Published in 2018 by The Rosen Publishing Group, Inc.
29 East 21st Street, New York, NY 10010

Editor: Theresa Morlock
Book Design: Michael Flynn
Interior Layout: Tanya Dellaccio

Photo Credits: Cover, pp. 9, 27 Hero Images/Getty Images; pp. 5, 25 Ariel Skelley/Blend Images/Getty Images; p. 6 vectorfusionart/Shutterstock.com; p. 7 Prostock-studio/Shutterstock.com; p. 10 Justin Sullivan/Getty Images News/Getty Images; p. 11 Blend Images - Hill Street Studios/Brand X Pictures/Getty Images; p. 12 Universal History Archive/Universal Images Group/Getty Images; p. 13 Everett Historical/Shutterstock.com; pp. 15, 16, 17 Bettmann/Getty Images; p. 19 Washington Bureau/Hulton Archive/Getty Images; p. 21 Pacific Press/LightRocket/Getty Images; pp. 22, 23 PAUL J. RICHARDS/AFP/Getty Images; p. 29 Africa Studio/Shutterstock.com.

Cataloging-in-Publication Data

Names: Almasy, Kip.
Title: Why voting matters / Kip Almasy.
Description: New York : PowerKids Press, 2018. | Series: Spotlight on civic action | Includes index.
Identifiers: ISBN 9781538327975 (pbk.) | ISBN 9781508163954 (library bound) | ISBN 9781538328095 (6 pack)
Subjects: LCSH: Voting--United States--Juvenile literature. | Elections--United States--Juvenile literature.
Classification: LCC JK1978.A46 2018 | DDC 324.60973--dc23

Manufactured in the United States of America

CPSIA Compliance Information: Batch #BW18PK For further information contact Rosen Publishing, New York, New York at 1-800-237-9932.

CONTENTS

THE POWER OF A VOTE 4
WHAT'S A CONSTITUENT? 6
VOTING RULES IN THE UNITED STATES 8
CAST YOUR BALLOT! 10
THE RIGHT TO VOTE 12
THE SUFFRAGISTS 14
AFRICAN AMERICAN DISENFRANCHISEMENT 16
THE VOTING RIGHTS ACT 18
THE NATIONAL VOTER REGISTRATION ACT 20
LOW VOTER TURNOUT 22
EXPLAINING LOW TURNOUT 24
IMPROVING VOTER TURNOUT 26
ACTIVE CITIZENSHIP 28
YOUR VOTE MATTERS 30
GLOSSARY 31
INDEX 32
PRIMARY SOURCE LIST 32
WEBSITES 32

CHAPTER ONE

THE POWER OF A VOTE

The right to vote is one of the most valuable rights an American citizen has. Voting is the process by which citizens elect government officials. Voting is also used to make decisions within the government. The U.S. Senate and House of Representatives make decisions by voting.

Casting a vote is a way to formally express your choice of representative or opinion about how the government operates. Without a vote, you have no voice and no influence in how decisions are made. Although there are millions of American citizens, every vote is important.

Throughout American history, certain groups have struggled to gain or exercise the right to vote. These people made many sacrifices to **guarantee** that, in the future, every American would have a voice in politics. The right to vote shouldn't be wasted or taken for granted.

The right to vote in an election is called suffrage.

CHAPTER TWO

WHAT'S A CONSTITUENT?

A constituent is a voting member of a community. Constituents vote to select representatives to speak for them at the local, state, and federal levels. Some examples of representatives include mayors, who are local representatives; state legislators, who are state representatives; and the president, who is a federal representative. Just as every vote is important, every election is important. The way leaders run each community can affect how leaders run the country as a whole.

The two main political parties in the United States are the Republican Party, which is represented by an elephant, and the Democratic Party, which is represented by a donkey.

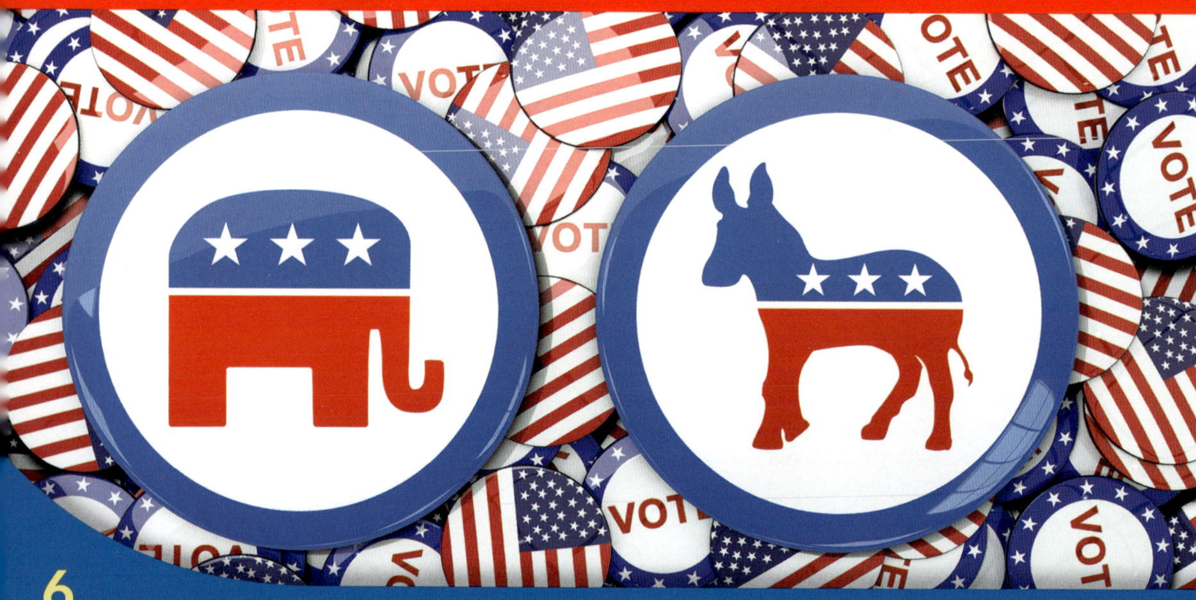

Today, political parties and candidates often publish their platforms online so citizens can read them. You can visit the website of a political party or candidate to learn about their platform.

No matter what kind of election you're voting in, it's important to be well informed about the candidates. Before you vote for a representative, research the actions they've taken in the past and what ideas they've proposed for the future. A candidate's plan or policy is called a platform. Careful voters find out what each candidate's platform is and decide which one is best for the country or area.

CHAPTER THREE

VOTING RULES IN THE UNITED STATES

A number of laws about voting exist in the United States. In order to vote, you must be a U.S. citizen. You must also be at least 18 years old. These are federal voting laws.

States also have voting laws. In most states, a person who has committed a felony, or serious crime, can't vote for a period of time. Some states require a person to live within the state for a certain time before they're allowed to vote there.

In most places, citizens have to register to vote at least several weeks before an election occurs. A person registers to vote by filling out a form with their name and address. States are divided into voting districts called precincts. Each precinct has places where citizens can go to vote. These are called polling places.

You can register to vote at the department of motor vehicles, at a local election office, or at a state public assistance office.

CHAPTER FOUR

CAST YOUR BALLOT!

The form you use to submit your vote is called a ballot. Ballots have a list of candidates for voters to choose from. Ballots are collected and counted in different ways. In some places, people vote using machines in private booths. In others, voters fill out a paper form. If you're not at your precinct at the time of

All voting in the United States is supposed to be free and private. However, this is not always the case.

an election, you can fill out a form called an absentee ballot and mail it in. After the votes are collected, they're counted by election officials or by computers.

Every person's vote is private. Each polling place sets up private booths or dividers so that nobody can read another person's ballot. Privacy protects voters from being threatened by people who don't agree with their choices. Voters are safer if every ballot is private. Most polling places are public buildings such as schools or fire halls.

CHAPTER FIVE

THE RIGHT TO VOTE

During the early years of the United States, most states allowed only white male property owners to vote. African American men weren't granted the right to vote until 1870, when the 15th Amendment was **ratified**. American women were denied the right to vote in many states until the 19th Amendment was ratified in 1920. American Indian people weren't allowed to vote until 1924.

The United States is founded on the idea that the government operates only with the consent, or permission and approval, of the people. Denying suffrage to certain groups of people robs them of their natural right of consent.

Susan B. Anthony, a champion of the women's suffrage movement, once said: "It was we, the people; not we, the white male citizens; nor yet we, the male citizens; but we, the whole people, who formed the Union. And we formed it, not to give the blessings of liberty, but to secure them; not to the half of ourselves and the half of our **posterity**, but to the whole people."

CHAPTER SIX

THE SUFFRAGISTS

Suffragists were people who fought to guarantee women the right to vote. The women's suffrage movement spanned from the late 1840s until 1920. Its beginning was marked by the Seneca Falls Convention of 1848 in Seneca Falls, New York. About 100 people attended the convention, during which Elizabeth Cady Stanton wrote the Declaration of Sentiments. This declaration outlined the goals of the women's rights movement, including the right to vote. In it, Stanton criticized the system of government that "compelled (each woman) to submit to laws, in the formation of which she had no voice."

Over the next century, suffragists would deal with arrest, mistreatment by the police, and government disregard before they'd win the right to vote. Some imprisoned suffragists used methods such as hunger strikes to raise awareness about their cause.

Stanton's declaration emphasized the idea that the right to vote is an inherent, or fundamental, human right.

CHAPTER SEVEN

AFRICAN AMERICAN DISENFRANCHISEMENT

Even after federal laws granted all citizens the right to vote, some states put laws and policies into place to prevent certain citizens from doing so.

The 15th Amendment of 1870 made it illegal to deny citizens the right to vote based on "race, color,

Being denied the right to vote is called disenfranchisement. In this photo, African Americans who had once been disenfranchised line up to vote in Alabama in 1966.

This photo taken in 1965 shows civil rights marchers at the Alabama state capitol protesting unfair voting laws.

or previous condition of servitude." However, in some southern states, officials passed unfair laws to keep African Americans from voting. Poll taxes required people to pay to be allowed to vote. Many African Americans were poor and could not afford the taxes. Reading tests were also used to keep people from voting. Many African Americans at the time had little formal education and couldn't pass these tests. African Americans also had to deal with threats from **white supremacists** who didn't want them to vote.

CHAPTER EIGHT

THE VOTING RIGHTS ACT

During the civil rights movement of the 1950s and 1960s, activists raised awareness about disenfranchisement and called for federal intervention to protect African Americans' voting rights. On August 6, 1965, the Voting Rights Act, or VRA, was signed into law. This law was designed to prevent racial **discrimination** in voting policies and practices.

The VRA helped thousands of disenfranchised people finally exercise their rights. This act proved to be very effective and has been renewed several times.

In 2006, the VRA was renewed again. Under two of the sections that must be renewed, assistance is provided to citizens whose first language isn't English, and monitors can be posted at polling places to make sure no one is turned away unfairly.

In this photo taken in 1965, President Lyndon B. Johnson gives civil rights leader Martin Luther King Jr. a pen used to sign the Voting Rights Act.

CHAPTER NINE

THE NATIONAL VOTER REGISTRATION ACT

In 1993, Congress passed another voting act. The National Voter Registration Act, or NVRA, was created to provide citizens with better voting opportunities. Under the terms of the act, states must offer citizens the chance to register to vote when they apply for a driver's license or renew their driver's license. States must also offer voter registration at state offices that provide public assistance or serve disabled people. The act also allows citizens to register to vote by mail.

The NVRA was intended to improve voter turnout. In its early days, several states objected to it and filed lawsuits against it. Multiple courts ruled that NVRA is constitutional, and the act is still in effect today.

Activists such as Darius Khalil Gordon, pictured on the right, continue to work to improve the voting process. Gordon is a community organizer for a group called Citizen Action of New York, which focuses on issues of inequality.

CHAPTER TEN

LOW VOTER TURNOUT

Although the United States has made many strides to make voter registration and the voting process more accessible to citizens, there is still a problem with people taking part. Voter turnout is key to a well-run **democracy**. The people run the United States government indirectly. When the people fail to

Voting is important to the democratic process. Can you think of any reasons for low voter turnout?

make their wants, needs, and opinions known to the government, the government can't serve them as well.

In recent presidential elections, about 60 percent of the qualified voting population in the United States has turned out to vote. Only about 40 percent take part in midterm elections. Voter turnout varies from state to state. Small states, such as New Hampshire, tend to have a higher rate of voter turnout than larger states, such as Texas.

CHAPTER ELEVEN

EXPLAINING LOW TURNOUT

There are many factors that affect voter turnout. For example, people are more likely to vote in a presidential election than a local one. Another factor that influences voter turnout is demographics. A demographic is a particular section of a population.

Citizens who are members of minority groups may be less likely to vote. A minority group is a group of people who are different from the larger group in their country in some way. Some examples of minority groups in the United States include African Americans and people with disabilities. Members of minority groups often have fewer people like themselves representing them in government. A minority person might not want to vote because they don't feel there's a candidate who represents their needs.

U.S. elections are decided by majority rule, which means the majority, or the group with more than half the people, has the power to elect U.S. leaders.

CHAPTER TWELVE

IMPROVING VOTER TURNOUT

To find solutions to low voter turnout, it's important to consider its causes. Some voters feel disconnected from politics and candidates. Other possible causes include work schedules that make it difficult or impossible to get to a polling place on time, or disabilities or physical conditions that make it difficult to travel.

Some ways to improve voter turnout may include simplifying the voting process, making it possible to vote from home, and promoting taking part in government throughout the year, not just on Election Day. Other solutions could be making it easier to register to vote or establishing universal voter registration, which means all adults would be automatically registered to vote. As the nation continues to grow and change, it's likely that our voting practices will, too.

What factors would make you more likely to vote?

CHAPTER THIRTEEN

ACTIVE CITIZENSHIP

Patriotism is the **devotion** that people have for their country. People show patriotism in many ways, but one of the most useful ways to express love for your country is to be an active citizen. Voting is an important part of being both an active citizen and a patriot.

How can you be an active citizen? Educate yourself about the history of your country. Reading the Declaration of Independence and the Constitution can help you learn about the ideas on which America was founded. It's also important to learn about current events. Think about how the founding ideas of democracy relate to what's going on in the world today. Even if you're too young to vote right now, you are the future of the United States.

Patriotism means more than waving a flag or saying the Pledge of Allegiance. True patriots think about how their country functions and what they could do to make it better in the future.

CHAPTER FOURTEEN

YOUR VOTE MATTERS

The Declaration of Independence says: "We hold these Truths to be **self-evident**, that all men are created equal," and that all men are born with "certain **unalienable** Rights." It continues: "to secure these rights, Governments are instituted among Men, **deriving** their just powers from the consent of the governed."

We the people of the United States have created our government to protect our natural-born rights. Our leaders receive their power from us, the citizens. Our representatives are only able to govern with our consent. Voting is the process by which we grant this consent.

Your vote matters because it's your voice in America's democracy. Your vote gives you the power to influence how your government is run. Use this freedom to create a better nation.

GLOSSARY

democracy (duh-MAH-kruh-see) A government elected by the people, directly or indirectly.

derive (dih-RYV) To take from a certain source.

devotion (dih-VOH-shun) Strong love, affection, or dedication to a person or country.

discrimination (dih-skrih-muh-NAY-shun) Different—usually unfair—treatment based on factors such as a person's race, age, religion, or gender.

guarantee (gayr-uhn-TEE) A formal promise that certain conditions will be fulfilled.

posterity (pah-STAYR-uh-tee) All future generations of people.

ratify (RAA-tih-fy) To formally approve something.

self-evident (SELF–EH-vuh-dunt) Obvious, something clear that doesn't need to be explained.

unalienable (uhn-AYL-yuh-nuh-buhl) Impossible to take away or give up.

white supremacist (WYT suh-PREH-muh-sist) A person who believes that white people are better than all other people.

INDEX

A
absentee ballot, 11
Alabama, 16, 17
Anthony, Susan, 13, 15

B
ballot, 10

C
Citizen Action of New York, 21
Congress, U.S., 20
constituent, 6
Constitution, U.S., 28

D
Declaration of Independence, 28, 30
Declaration of Sentiments, 14, 15
Democratic Party, 6
demographics, 24
disenfranchisement, 16, 18

F
15th Amendment, 12, 16

G
Gordon, Darius Khalil, 21

H
House of Representatives, U.S., 4

J
Johnson, Lyndon B., 19

K
King, Martin Luther, Jr., 19

M
majority rule, 25

N
National Voter Registration Act, 20
New Hampshire, 23
New York, 14, 21
19th Amendment, 12

P
patriotism, 28, 29
platform, 7
political parties, 6, 7
polling places, 8, 11
poll taxes, 17
precincts, 8, 10

R
Republican Party, 6

S
Senate, U.S., 4
Seneca Falls Convention, 14
Stanton, Elizabeth Cady, 14, 15
suffrage, 5, 12, 13, 14
suffragists, 14

T
Texas, 23
turnout, 20, 22, 23, 24, 26

V
Voting Rights Act, 18, 19

PRIMARY SOURCE LIST

Page 13
Susan B. Anthony. Photograph. ca 1890 and 1910. Created by Frances Benjamin Johnston. Now kept at the Library of Congress, Prints and Photographs Division, Washington, D.C.

Page 15
Susan B. Anthony and Elizabeth Cady Stanton. Photograph. ca. 1891. Created by Edmonston. Now kept at the Library of Congress, Records of the National Women's Party, Washington, D.C.

Page 19
President Lyndon B. Johnson hands Martin Luther King Jr. a pen. Photograph. August 6, 1965. Created by United Press International Photograph. Now kept at the Library of Congress, Prints and Photographs Division, Washington, D.C.

WEBSITES

Due to the changing nature of Internet links, PowerKids Press has developed an online list of websites related to the subject of this book. This site is updated regularly. Please use this link to access the list: www.powerkidslinks.com/sociv/voting